Harry Pottiness...

'I've never laughed so much!'
Derrick the Dementor

'Siriusly funny stuff!'
S. Black

'Purr-fect...'
Crookshanks

'More fun than a barrelful of Blast-Ended Skrewts.'
Rubeus Hagrid

'I couldn't stop howling!'
Fluffy

'Ha ha, very funny.'
You Know Who

PUFFIN BOOKS

Published by the Penguin Group
Penguin Books Ltd, 80 Strand, London WC2R 0RL, England
Penguin Group (USA), Inc., 375 Hudson Street, New York, New York 10014, USA
Penguin Books Australia Ltd, 250 Camberwell Road, Camberwell, Victoria 3124, Australia
Penguin Books Canada Ltd, 10 Alcorn Avenue, Toronto, Ontario, Canada M4V 3B2
Penguin Books India (P) Ltd, 11 Community Centre, Panchsheel Park, New Delhi – 110 017, India
Penguin Group (NZ), cnr Airborne and Rosedale Roads, Albany, Auckland 1310, New Zealand
Penguin Books (South Africa) (Pty) Ltd, 24 Sturdee Avenue, Rosebank 2196, South Africa

Penguin Books Ltd, Registered Offices: 80 Strand,
London WC2R 0RL, England

www.penguin.com

First published 2004

3

Written by Richard Dungworth
Illustrated by Martin Chatterton

With love and thanks to Naomi and Greg

Set in Aunt Mildred

Made and printed in England by Clays Ltd, St Ives plc

British Library Cataloguing in Publication Data
A CIP catalogue record for this book is available from the British Library

ISBN 0–141–31847–3

Harry Pottiness

a Totally Unofficial

Book of Muggle Fun

Contents

Where did Dobby learn tai-kwon-do?

At elf-defence classes.

What's utterly terrifying and carries a bricklaying trowel?

A Cementor.

Where is the best place to drink Polyjuice Potion?

In a changing room.

What secret language do postal workers use?

Parceltongue.

Is it hard to tell
Professors McGonagall
and Trelawny apart?

No, it's easy to tell which
witch is which.

HARRY: 'Why are
you sucking throat
lozenges?'

FIRENZE: 'I'm a bit
horse.'

How do feverish, congested
wizards get around?

They use the Flu Network.

Which spell
gets rid
of B. O.?

Exsmelliarmus.

'We apologize to passengers on Platform Nine and Three Quarters awaiting the delayed 11 o'clock service to Hogwarts. This service is now running approximately two-and-a-half weeks late, following a Time Turner incident in the Uttoxeter area.'

'Will the owner of a large brown carnivorous suitcase please go *immediately* to the Lost Magical Property Office. Passengers are requested *not* to leave aggressive luggage unattended.'

'This is a platform change announcement. Due to new Ministry regulations, Platform Nine and Three Quarters will in future be referred to as Platform Nine Point Seven Five.'

Platform Nine and Three Quarters

'Ghosts and other undead boarding the *Hogwarts Express* are advised that the buffet trolley is *not* licensed to serve spirits. Recently-cremated passengers should please use the Smoking Carriage provided at the rear of the train.'

'All passengers planning to board the 11.30 "Master Gaoler" service to Azkaban should have reservations. I know I would.'

'Animagi wishing to travel to Hogwarts School of Witchcraft and Wizardry should change here.'

Simply Divine!

We asked Divination expert Sybil Trelawny to take a look at a selection of drained teacups, to see what the tea leaves revealed about each drinker's future. Here's what she had to say...

Cedric Diggory's cuppa

'Your future is bright and full of fun. I forecast that you *will* be invited to your second cousin's Hallowe'en brunch, where you will win the Every Flavour Beans in the Tombola.'

Cho Chang's cuppa

'Hmmm, a complex pattern, but one that clearly indicates, I'm afraid, that you will be involved in a freak Occulomency accident, somewhere in the Midlands, on or around Shrove Tuesday.'

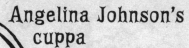

Angelina Johnson's cuppa

'Aha – The Lovers' Knot! I'm seeing – yes, it's becoming clear now – you will meet a Muggle Relations Officer with a wooden leg during a hailstorm. It's hard to be certain but – yes – the leaves tell me that the two of you will adopt a flobberworm.'

Harry Potter's cuppa

'Well, I think this one speaks for itself, don't you? Quite obvious...'

Hermione Granger's cuppa

'I'm good, but even I can't work with teabags, dear.'

11

What's large and
hairy with a single
fang?
Hagrid.

What did Hedwig say when
Harry forgot to write on an
envelope?
'Twit! To who?'

RON: 'I've just eaten twenty-
four Chocolate Frogs!'
HARRY: 'How do you feel?'
RON: 'Extremely hoppy.'

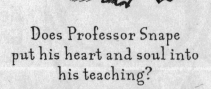

Does Professor Snape
put his heart and soul into
his teaching?

No, he just goes through
the potions.

What's packed
with flowers,
but full of danger?

The Forbidden
Florists.

What do you call it
when Fawkes phones up
for a takeaway?

The Order of the
Phoenix.

How do wizards protect their skin
from hot sun?

With suntan potion.

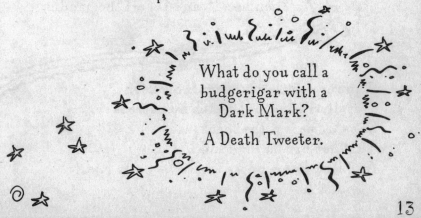

What do you call a
budgerigar with a
Dark Mark?

A Death Tweeter.

Hooray for Hogwarts!

There once was a Slytherin Beater,
Who was truly the most *dreadful* cheater.
If another team's Chaser
Could clearly outpace her,
She'd change to a dragon, and eat her.

A Gryffindor Keeper called Wood,
Used to practise whenever he could,
So that whereas before,
He'd let anyone score,
He is now, to be frank, jolly good.

There once was a Chaser called Randall,
Whose temper caused many a scandal.
He would loop, swoop and zoom
On his super-cool broom,
Then lose it, and fly off the handle.

A young female Hufflepuff Seeker,
Was distracted mid-match by a streaker.
So extreme was the shock,
That her broom ran amok,
And flew her — guess where? — Costa Rica!

A Hogwarts professor called Lupin
Could do nothing to stop his wand drooping.
Then one day (in March),
He fixed it, with starch,
And ran around joyfully whooping.

A Potions professor named Snape,
Was reluctant to use Spellotape,
As he'd once got entrapped
In a gift that he'd wrapped,
And taken ten hours to escape.

A Herbology teacher called Sprout,
Had to ask all her students to shout,
As over the years
She'd got soil in her ears,
And now couldn't get it back out.

A 'charming' professor named Flitwick,
Was in fact an intolerant critic.
He would give students hell
If they messed up a spell
And would endlessly fault-find and nitpick.

Invisibility Cloak Care Label

95% Demiguise hair, 5% lycra
Colour: none
Size: one-size only
Maximum coverage: two children and a crated dragon

  Please wash separately. Invisibility pigment may run, causing other garments to become blurred or transparent.

 Do not iron. What's the point — nobody will see the creases ...

 Do not bleach or dye. Frankly, why would you want to?

⚠ KEEP AWAY FROM DRAGON FIRE.

Congratulations

on becoming the proud owner of a ThinAir Invisibility Cloak! Woven from only the finest Demiguise hair, this classic garment is one you'll want to not be seen in for many years to come. All ThinAir cloaks are covered by a lifetime guarantee (provided you're not immortal).

Please note that ThinAir cloaks only hide the visible. Smells and sounds are *not* disguised. The manufacturers therefore advise against the consumption of baked beans or curried eggs prior to a venture during which detection is undesired.

Important Safety Notice

Individuals using their Invisibility Cloak while cycling should ensure that they wear an appropriate hi-visibility safety vest.

ThinAir
for quality you just can't see.

What did Salazar Slytherin
keep under his bed?

The Chamber Pot of Secrets.

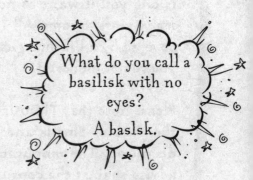

What do you call a
basilisk with no
eyes?

A baslsk.

What lurks
underwater and gives
off smelly bubbles?

A Windylow.

What soccer position
does Firenze play?

Centaur forward.

What spell should you use
if someone attacks you with
a shopping catalogue?
ExpelliArgos.

What does Nicolas
Flamel cook his
dinner in?
The Philosopher's Stove.

What does Harry
like on his chips?
HP Sauce.

How do mountain
trolls like to spend
their evenings?
Clubbing.

What's in a name?

Ever since the infamous
TOM MARVOLO RIDDLE = I AM LORD VOLDEMORT
incident, it's been clear that wizards – even
thoroughly evil ones – enjoy a bit of wordplay. As
future adventures unfold, be on the lookout for
characters whose names can be reshuffled into
something more sinister...

Name: **Trevor Oldmold**
Description: Doddering geriatric
gardener taken on
at Hogwarts
Unscrambled
Identity: Yikes! LORD
VOLDEMORT

Name: **Todd Harlerk**
Description: Pleasant Scottish
delivery boy
Unscrambled
Identity: Oh dear, it's...
THE DARK LORD

Name: Dr Dermot Vollo

Description: Madame Pomfrey's charming new assistant

Unscrambled Identity: a.k.a. LORD VOLDEMORT

Name: Mr Lovedot

Description: The Dursleys' friendly new neighbour

Unscrambled Identity: You guessed it! VOLDEMORT again

Name: Ben Dowth, The Mouse-Man

Description: Famous travelling Animagus

Unscrambled Identity: Surely not... HE WHO MUST NOT BE NAMED

You get the idea. Be vigilant. Trust no one, and you might just make it to the end of Book Seven. Mr V. will keep turning up as someone, somewhere, or my name's not **Mel Drovot**...

TOP OF THE POTTER POPS

This week's Wizard Chart,
compiled by Codswallup.

Three songs going down, two going up, three new
Apparations and two non-movers (due to an
accident involving the Petrificus Totalus curse).

1 'Can't Get You Out of My Head'
Professor Quirrell

2 'Cry Me A River' *(HIGHEST NEW APPARITION!)*
Moaning Myrtle

3 'Cleanin' Out My Closet'
Dobby and the House Elves

4 'Hootylicious'
Hedwig and Pig

5 'Who Let the Dogs Out?'
DJ Fluffy

6 'Scandalous'
Rita Skeeter

7 'It Wasn't Me'
Fred 'n' George

8 'Flying Without Wings'
Firebolt 2000

9 'Dancing in the Moonlight'
Remus 'The Prof' Lupin

10 'Spinning Around'
Aragog and the Web Weavers

Songs for the Knight Bus

Ten wizard ditties to help you pass the journey with Ernie...

'If You're Harry And You Know It ...'

'How Much Is That Broomstick In The Window?'

'Umbridge Is Falling Down'

'Old McGonagall Had A Charm'

'The Hocus Pocus Kokey'

'Norbert, The Magic Dragon'

'My Old Man's An Auror'

'Who's Afraid Of The Big Bad Werewolf?'

'The Wheels On The Knight Bus'

'There's A Hole In My Cauldron'

HARRY: 'Hedwig's lost her voice.'
HERMIONE: 'Oh, dear – is she terribly upset?'
HARRY: 'Nah, she doesn't give a hoot...'

What do wizards wear at the seaside?

Curse-me-quick hats.

Did you hear about the wizard who got trapped in Gringotts Bank?

The Goblins insisted it was someone else's vault.

Who wears a turban and likes nuts?

That's Quirrell.

Which wizard
is very powerful,
but extremely dull?

Albus Dumblebore.

Which Death Eater has
trouble keeping his
sunglasses on?

Loose-ears Malfoy.

Is being a
Dementor
a fun job?

No, it's soul-
destroying.

Which ghost works on
the Hogwarts Express?

The Ticket Inspectre.

Ask Hagrid

As always, your owls have been flocking into the Big Man himself here at *Magical Creature Enthusiast*. Here's what he had to say in answer to three of our readers' queries:

Dear Hagrid

I acquired a young Hippogriff, called Buttbeak, over a year ago, and have since been looking forward to riding him in flight. However, he has yet to show any inclination to become airborne, preferring to wallow in mud and laze about. His rear quarters are also assuming alarming proportions, and I'm concerned that he is becoming too ungainly ever to leave the ground.

Imelda Splot

Dear Imelda

I been scratchin' my 'ead abou' this one for a while now. What I reckon is you ain't got yourself no Hippogriff there. What you gone and got is an hippopotamus.

Dear Hagrid

I've been an avid dragon breeder for over twenty years, but have recently come across the most unusual find of my career. I'm now the proud owner of an unhatched dragon's egg unlike any I have seen before: large, smooth to the touch, more spherical than the typical egg, and remarkable for its shell markings — segments of bright, primary colours. Do you have any thoughts on what species or variety it might contain, or how to stimulate hatching?

Jerimiah Jinks

Dear Jerimiah

By the sounds of it, I'd say you'd been 'ad, lad. You're the proud owner o' one of them beach balls.

Dear Hagrid

I've been raising a Blast-Ended Skrewt for some months now, and have been following your instructions [see Issue 17] as to how best to approach it so as to avoid injury. However, every attempt so far has led to my sustaining serious burns, and the staff at St Mungo's are beginning to joke about my being 'one of their regulars'. What am I doing wrong?

Ramona Portley

Dear Ramona

You don't 'ave a Blast-Ended Skrewt, but one o' those rarer Blast-Sided varieties. Get down on your 'ands and knees, come at the dear little thing from the front and see 'ow you get on.

Rubeus Hagrid

Bogus Bookshelf

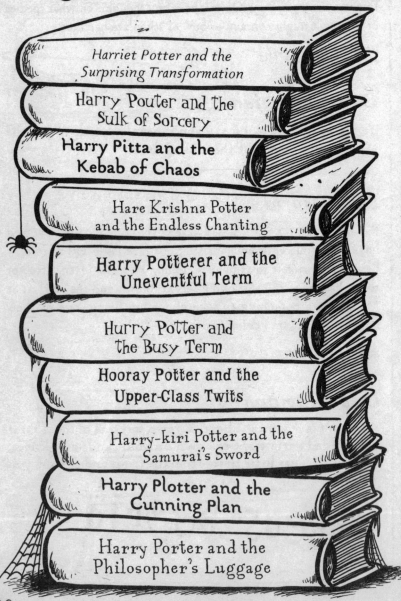

Harriet Potter and the
Surprising Transformation

Harry Pouter and the
Sulk of Sorcery

Harry Pitta and the
Kebab of Chaos

Hare Krishna Potter
and the Endless Chanting

Harry Potterer and the
Uneventful Term

Hurry Potter and
the Busy Term

Hooray Potter and the
Upper-Class Twits

Harry-kiri Potter and the
Samurai's Sword

Harry Plotter and the
Cunning Plan

Harry Porter and the
Philosopher's Luggage

Everyone wants to know the title of the next book. Here are some of our (very) wild guesses...

Harry Blotter and the Stain of Doom

Harry Otter and the Animagus Potion

Hairy Potter and the Werewolf's Bite

Harry Plantpotter and the Pansies of Peril

Kalahari Potter and the Desert of Despair

Harry TrainsPotter and the Tannoy of Terror

'Arry Potter and the Cockney Conjuror

Parry Hotter and the Spelling Nightmare

HARRY PUTTER AND THE GOLFING GOBLIN

Harry Popper and the Balloons of Bewilderment

When is it best to keep away from Hagrid?

When he's got a Skrewt loose.

What has the head and wings of an eagle, the body of a horse, but only one leg?

A hoppogriff.

PROF. TRELAWNY: 'You will die. You will die. You will die. You will die.'
HARRY: 'Why do you keep repeating yourself, Miss?'
PROF. TRELAWNY: 'I'm four-telling the future.'

Where does the Knight Bus give way to other traffic?

At the Magic Roundabout.

With what can you clean up the secret tunnels at Hogwarts?

The Marauder's Mop.

What's stunningly beautiful, but likely to rip you off?

A wheeler-dealer Veela.

Which famous Auror has a false eye and no clothes?

Mad-Eye Noody.

Do Phoenixes use cutlery?

Just Fawkes.

The *Sunday Sorceror* Lonely Hearts Page

♥ Game-for-a-laugh gamekeeper, tall (very), dark and hairy, seeks XXL companion for moonlit walks in Forbidden Forest. Must be a pet-lover.

♥ Off-duty prison guard, ice-cool, strong and silent type, wicked kisser, seeks soul-mate. Appearances unimportant. No chocoholics.

♥ Once bitten, twice shy ex-professor, wolfish good-looks, active night life, seeks she-wolf to help him cope with changes in his life.

♥ Retired lady, former High Inquisitor, no sense of humour, seeks short-sighted, desperate or reptilian companion for candlelit (or, if preferred, unlit) dinners.

♥ Tall, dark and handy-with-a-cauldron professor would like to meet like-minded lady to share his home-brewed potions.

♥ Lonely, misunderstood megalomaniac seeks parselmouth partner, good hisser, for eternal friendship, maybe more. Pure-bloods only.

♥ Your bathroom or mine? Young woman with cheerless disposition seeks partner to stay in with. Must be a good listener in need of a steady ghoul-friend.

♥ Good-looking, successful, modest author wishes to meet someone special to discover new interests. Can't remember old ones. Should live within travelling distance of St Mungo's.

Ten Ways to Annoy the Dark Lord

1 Draw a lightning-bolt scar on his forehead while he's asleep.

2 Buy him tickets for *Potter: The Musical*.

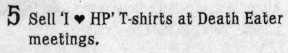

3 Ask him how his folks are.

4 Call him 'Voldie'.

5 Sell 'I ♥ HP' T-shirts at Death Eater meetings.

6 Book him on an Anger Management course.

7 Hum the tune to 'I ain't got no body' whenever you're with him.

8 Hide his wand.

9 Ask him if the Dark Mark couldn't be made a bit, you know, more attractive.

10 Tell him frequently to 'cheer up'.

Ten Ways to Annoy Hermione

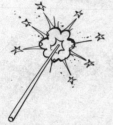

1 Call her 'Hermee-own'.

2 Suggest that she change the name of the 'Society for the Promotion of Elfish Welfare' to 'Promoters of Universal Kindness to Elves'.

3 Criticize her Charms homework essay, as you copy it.

4 Scratch HG ♥ VK on her wand.

5 Correct her Latin pronunciation.

6 Play a tune on your teeth when she's trying to study.

7 Say, 'Well, if you love Herbology, why don't you *marry* it?'

8 Shuffle her numerically organized Arithmancy crib cards.

9 Give Crookshanks her Time Turner to play with.

10 Fold up her OWL revision timetable to make a water-bomb.

What do wizards use
to improve the
weather?

Sunny spells.

Why does Mr Dursley
refuse to believe in
Dobby?

He's in elf-denial.

What do
Dementors do
at the
weekend?

Just chill.

What's huge,
leafy and rather
pathetic?

The Whimpering
Willow.

Is Harry's godfather
game for a laugh?

No, he's always
Sirius.

RON: 'How much were your
Chudley Cannons tickets?'

SEAMUS: 'Quid each.'

Why do Thestrals make
terrible liars?

You can see right
through them.

Did you hear the one
about the self-conscious
Boggart?

He didn't like
changing in public.

UNEMPLOYED? JOBS AVAILABLE NOW!

Monster-movie extras needed. 10 Galleons/hr. Must have a face like a bulldog chewing a wasp. Contact Nathan @ Gross-out Films.

Send owl Monday

finish Knitting Potter Voodoo doll

take corset to be reinforced

ALSO, AVAILABLE SOON...

The Mirror of Yrettalf

Bye-bye troll-chops, hellooooo Veela-lady! This uplifting mirror magically edits out crow's feet, nostril hairs, warts and all, to reflect you the way you'd love to look.

Fantastic for that first early morning peek

The Mirror of Rethgual

Turns your bathroom into a laugh-room!

See your funny side with this laugh-a-minute looking glass. You'll soon see how much fun cleaning your teeth is when you have a clown's nose, or shaving when you've got a handlebar moustache.

What do you call
Professor McGonagall
trapped between
two layers of bread?

A sandwitch.

Why wasn't
Voldemort
at the Yule Ball?

He had no body
to go with.

What type of car
flies best?

A budgericar.

What's full of
litter and
guarded
by Dementors?

Azkabin.

How does Aragog
communicate with
distant friends?

By Webcam.

Which famous trophy
was created by a
dragon's sneeze?

The Gobbet of Fire.

What do you call a wizard
who's a hit with the ladies?

A smooth Apparator.

How many mountain trolls
does it take to screw in a
lightbulb?

Four. One to hold the bulb still,
the other three to turn the
ceiling round.

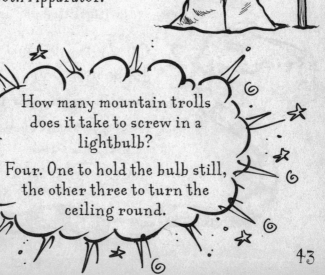

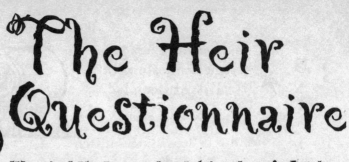

The Heir Questionnaire

Worried that your best friend **might** be the Heir of Slytherin? Run this quick-and-easy ten-part checklist, and you'll soon know for sure . . .

1 Are your friend's eyes:
a) bright blue, with long lashes?
b) dark brown, with hazel flecks?
c) fiery red, with slitted pupils?

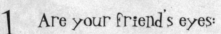

2 On your birthday, did he give you:
a) a Honeydukes selection box?
b) a Chudley Cannons poster?
c) a peculiar skull-and-snake tattoo on your forearm?

44

3 Ask him what he'd like for his birthday. Does he say:
a) 'a surprise'?
b) 'anything to do with Quidditch'?
c) 'eternal life'?

4 When he falls over, does he:
a) make a big fuss?
b) jump up and get on with things?
c) tell you, rather solemnly, that he 'will rise again'?

5 If he has a pet, is it:
a) a goldfish?
b) a gerbil?
c) a basilisk?

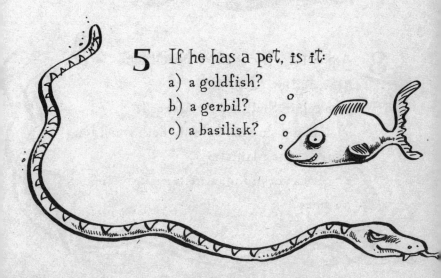

6 Ask him to say 'Hello!' in another language. Does he respond:
a) 'Bonjour!'?
b) 'Guten Tag!'?
c) 'Sssssssfthfthssssssss!'?

7 What does he prefer you to call him?
a) a special nickname?
b) 'mate'?
c) 'My Lord'?

8 Ask him why you've never met his family. Does he:
a) explain that they live abroad?
b) tell you that his parents both work long hours at the Ministry?
c) give a very long, sinister laugh, and say no more?

9 Tell him that you're going to study Unicorns next in Care of Magical Creatures. Does he:

a) tell you that he is allergic to animal hair?

b) say 'Aahhh ... cute ...'?

c) lick his lips?

10 If a fellow student has Muggle parents, does your friend:

a) treat her just like anyone else?

b) quiz her about Muggle habits?

c) mutter 'Foul Mudblood' under his breath whenever she's around?

How did you do?

If you answered mostly 'c', you should not, under any circumstances, borrow your friend's diary, tease him about his unusual middle name, or show him your interesting scar. And you should probably leave the country immediately.

How does Hedwig
plan a journey?

With a hootfinder.

What drink does the kiosk
on Platform Nine and
Three Quarters sell?

Hogwarts Espresso.

What do you get if
you cross a Dementor
with a wizard?

A cold spell.

Where does Dobby
buy lentils?

At an elf-food shop.

What's the best kind of friend to help you brew a potion?

One cauld-ron.

What drains your soul of happiness, and smells of Polos?

A Demintor.

Where does Professor Lupin live?

In a werehouse.

Where do Death Eaters do their discount shopping?

The Dark Mart.

PowerOwl
the wise choice

→ Fed up with being let down by the Owl Post?

→ Feathered friend more 'twit' then 'twoo'?

→ Be wise – get your talons on a PowerOwl, the all-new hi-tech messaging system for the up-to-the-minute wizard.

Say goodbye to painful perching with PowerOwl's **SoftGrip** talons!

'Reliable post, without all that hooting – highly recommended.'
Wiz-Tech Weekly

- PowerOwl's automatic Howler Filter means no more embarrassing moments in public.

- Sending a magical potion recipe or incantation? PowerOwl's hi-tech SpellChecker feature will help you avoid unfortunate mistakes.

- No need for dried mice or drinking bowls. The NightOwl base unit will recharge your PowerOwl's lithium battery while you sleep.

- No messy pellets or feather-shedding. PowerOwl is clean and maintenance-free.

51

Bluff Your Way

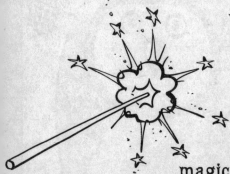

You may think it's a dead-boring dead language, but if you want to get on in the wizarding world, Latin is a must. To maintain your credibility as a magical adventurer, find out how to translate any command into an 'authentic' Latin-sounding version — in four easy steps...

STEP 1
Remove any instances of the words a, an or the:

change into a gigantic frog

STEP 2
Move describing words to go after the thing they describe, rather than before:

change into frog gigantic

in Magical Latin

STEP 3

If a word ends with one or more vowels
(a, e, i, o or u), remove these letters:

chang~~e~~ int~~o~~ frog gigantic

STEP 4

Now add one of the endings
from the box below to each word:

atis	ae	emus	ior	itis	ius
	ia	orum	ori	um	us

chang<u>ior</u> int<u>ae</u> frog<u>orum</u> gigant<u>icus</u>

Hey presto! (or rather
'heyus prestemus!') – you
have your Latin phrase.*

---

*The publishers accept no responsibility for any personal injuries or
damage to magical property caused by spells cast in Bluffer's Latin.

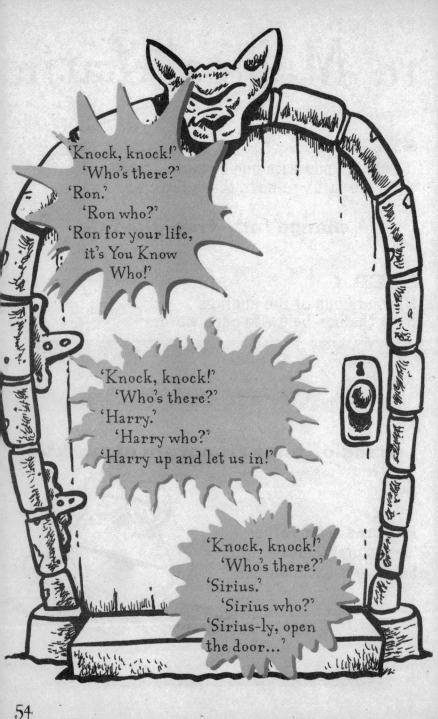

'Knock, knock!'
'Who's there?'
'Ron.'
'Ron who?'
'Ron for your life,
it's You Know
Who!'

'Knock, knock!'
'Who's there?'
'Harry.'
'Harry who?'
'Harry up and let us in!'

'Knock, knock!'
'Who's there?'
'Sirius.'
'Sirius who?'
'Sirius-ly, open
the door...'

54

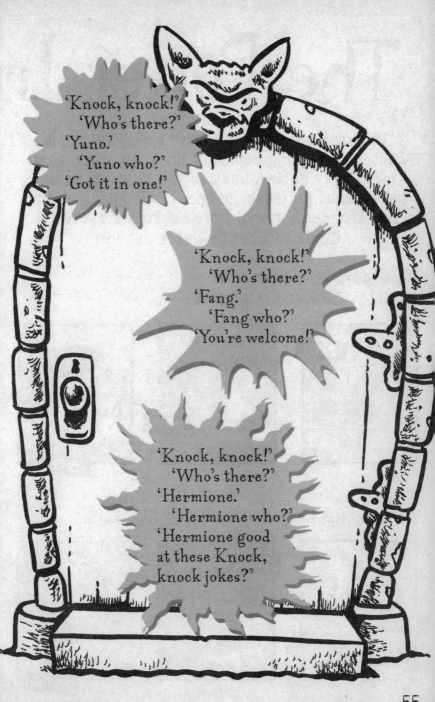

The Potter Im

The chap opening your town's new shopping centre, or signing copies of Book Six, may **say** he's Harry Potter, but can you be sure? Be on the lookout for lesser magical folk posing as the Boy Wonder himself. Here's a Potter Spotter's Guide to what to watch out for:

Glasses:
Should be plain, round-rimmed:

Scar:
Should be lightning-bolt shaped, on forehead:

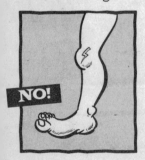  

postor Spotter

Wand:
Should be eleven inches long, made of holly:

Other Giveaways:
➜ wooden leg
➜ metal hook for hand
➜ he introduces his parents
➜ 'he' pops to the
    girls' toilet

The Real McCoy ➜
Finally, here's a picture
of the genuine article,
complete with his trademark
Invisibility Cloak.

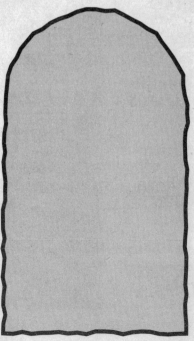

The Ghostly Gazette

Peeves' Puzzle Page

Our resident poltergeist has jumbled up a whole host of familiar names. See if you can pair up each character with its scrambled version. It'll haunt you until you do ...

SEVERUS
SNAPE

HERMIONE
GRANGER

MAD RACY FOOL

CROOKEDLY ALRIGHT

SAVE UP SNEERS

DRACO
MALFOY

CALM LOVING MANAGER

GILDEROY
LOCKHART

SLYLY RUDE DUDE

OLD DEER BUM

MINERVA
MCGONAGALL

SLIPPER SUNROOF

DUDLEY
DURSLEY

MEAN HERRING OGRE

PETUNIA
DURSLEY

EASILY UPTURNED

PROFESSOR
LUPIN

DUMBLEDORE

After a lot of cajoling and stroking of wings, we managed to get our old friend the Sphinx to provide one of its trademark riddles for our second puzzle.

See if you can unravel its clever-clogs clues to reveal the only creature that even Hagrid thinks is too revolting to care for ...

My **first** appears in 'Nimbus', but is not in 'Mr Binns'.

My **second** is in 'Hermione', but is not in 'heroine'.

My **third** is found in 'Dobby', but is not in 'Draco Malfoy'.

My **fourth** appears in 'Sirius', but is not in 'stupid boy'.

My **fifth** comes twice in 'basilisk', but isn't found in 'snake'.

My **sixth** is midway in 'middle', as it is in 'firedrake'.

My **seventh** is in 'Hagrid', but is not in 'so I heard'.

My **eighth** is found in 'Beater', but in neither 'bat' nor 'bird'.

ANSWER: Oh no! It's that UMBRIDGE woman again ...

Is Percy Harry's best friend?

No, wrong Weasley.

Which of Voldemort's henchmen is as daft as a brush?

Peter Pottygrew.

Which spell will make a toilet light up?

Loomos.

What lives in the fridge and exploits your worst fears?

A Boggart yoghurt.

What does Professor Moody put on a cut?

An Alastorplast.

What has fourteen legs and can't fly for toffee?

The Hufflepuff Quidditch team.

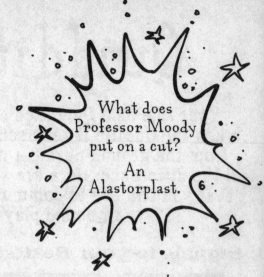

How do you kill a basilisk?

With a knife and Fawkes.

What lies on the floor of Voldemort's barber's?

The Hair of Slytherin.

Quidditch Coa

Your role as a Quidditch coach isn't over when the Quaffle is released. Tactical advice from the ground during a match can make all the difference. Here are some basic signals that you can use to communicate with your air-bound players.

Signals to your Beaters and Chasers:

'Assume an attacking formation'

'Assume a defensive formation'

'Forget it – just get the Quaffle, please'

'We need to move up'

'We need to drop back'

'We need a miracle'

ching Signals

Signals to your Keeper:

'Cover the
left/right
goal-post'

'Cover the
central
goal-post'

'Let in another
and your owl
gets it'

Signals to your Seeker:

'The Snitch is
right behind
you, you idiot'

DEMENTOR
APPLICATION FORM

NAME

Derrick Mentor

ADDRESS

13 Despair Drive, Chillington,
Soulless-on-Sea UR1 2IC

POST APPLIED FOR

Assistant Guard, Azkaban Detention Centre

QUALIFICATIONS

NVQ Level 1 in Rattling Breathing

Black Cross Certificate in Soul-Sucking

Pursuing Night Release course to gain Anti-Patronus
Certification, Bronze Level

RSA Grade 1, Typing and wordprocessing

EMPLOYMENT HISTORY

I am currently employed as Senior Air Chiller at EasyFreeze, a frozen-food company in Basingstoke.

In my previous job as a confectionery sales representative, I helped to increase sales of all chocolate lines by over 200%.

I have also worked in TV, appearing in a number of hand-cream commercials as the 'Before' man, and as a Traffic warden.

PERSONAL INFORMATION

My hobbies and interests include a number of solo winter sports, cross-stitch, and bringing terror and hopelessness into the lives of the unsuspecting.

I am the current Treasurer for the Society for the Scaly Skinned. I enjoy music, particularly soul or anything by Coldplay, and play the banjo to Grade 6.

What's fast, spotty and practises the Dark Arts?

A Death Cheetah.

Which broomstick is the absolute pits?

The Direbolt.

Why does Dobby keep criticizing himself?

He has low elf-esteem.

What spell should you use against rampaging vegetables?

Stewpify.

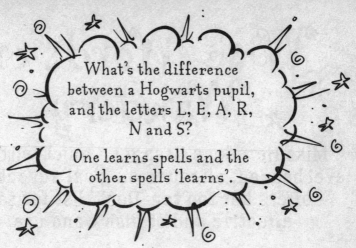

What's the difference between a Hogwarts pupil, and the letters L, E, A, R, N and S?

One learns spells and the other spells 'learns'.

Who puts out the candles in the girls' dormitory at Hogwarts?

The lightswitch.

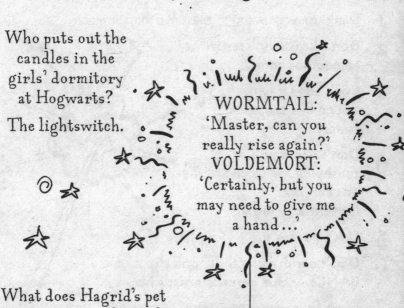

WORMTAIL: 'Master, can you really rise again?'
VOLDEMORT: 'Certainly, but you may need to give me a hand...'

What does Hagrid's pet spider wear in the pool?

Aragoggles.

Wise Words on Wandery

Miss Hermione Granger – quick-witted, level-headed, all-round magical adventuress – offers her top ten 'Don't' list for safe, effective and stylish wand use.

1 Don't use your wand to toast marshmallows on.

2 **Don't knit a holster for it (soooo not cool).**

3 Don't leave it lying around in a chopstick factory.

4 **Don't use it as a toothpick, or to clean out earwax (potentially lethal).**

5 Don't sharpen it.

6 **Don't conduct with it (one slip and – BANG! – your percussionist's history...)**

7 Don't fit it with a key ring.

8 **Don't chew its ends.**

9 Don't hand over your wand to a hooded stranger with a low, rasping voice who says that he'd 'just like to have a look at it for a minute'.

10 **Don't keep it down your underwear.**

The Swiss Army Wand

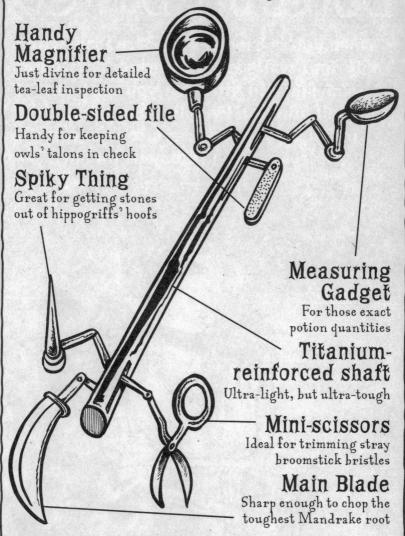

Handy Magnifier
Just divine for detailed tea-leaf inspection

Double-sided file
Handy for keeping owls' talons in check

Spiky Thing
Great for getting stones out of hippogriffs' hoofs

Measuring Gadget
For those exact potion quantities

Titanium-reinforced shaft
Ultra-light, but ultra-tough

Mini-scissors
Ideal for trimming stray broomstick bristles

Main Blade
Sharp enough to chop the toughest Mandrake root

'The ultimate all-round wand for the more adventurous wizard or witch.'

Wanda McWunda, *The Witches' Guide To Wands*

Boredom Busters

When you're banged up in Azkaban, with only four walls and a Dementor or two for company, it's vital that you can keep yourself amused. Here are some great ways to fill those prison days, courtesy of Azkaban's most infamous inmate.

1 Collect your belly-button fluff. When you have enough, knit finger-puppets of Voldemort and Dumbledore and enact an epic battle.

2 Stage a left-hand-versus-right-hand 'Scissors, Paper, Stone' tournament.

3 Chase your tail.*

4 Begin digging an escape tunnel in the stone floor with your thumbnail.

5 Befriend the spider that shares your cell. Try to learn its language.

6 Try out new, daring styles for your facial hair.

7 Make up a funny rhyme including the words 'avada kedavra', 'balaclava' and 'guava'.

8 Spend an hour or two licking your back leg.*

9 Fashion a fake wand from earwax. Wave it menacingly at your Dementor guards. Laugh if they flinch.

10 Compose your own musical score using only armpit noises.

*suggestion applies only to Animagi

In which Muggle city do most female magicians live?

Ipswitch.

What do you call a boy with a lightning-bolt scar and a lighthouse on his head?

Flash Harry.

Which frightful Hogwarts ghost is old-fashioned and in need of a wash?

The fuddy-duddy muddy Bloody Baron.

Why is Norbert the Norwegian Ridgeback a poor after-dinner speaker?

He tends to drag on.

Why was Mad-Eye Moody asked to resign?

He couldn't control his pupils.

What did Harry say when he saw Viktor clone himself?

'Krums!'

Why isn't Mr Ollivander much good at conversation?

He has a wand-track mind.

What has a list and a trolley and can see into the future?

A shopping centaur.

You'd have to be Knuts...

...to pay good Galleons for these farSickle articles!

SELF-COMBUSTING!

Fawkes the Phoenix model kit

Assemble the individual components to build this impressive life-size replica of Dumbledore's feathered friend. Then watch and wonder as it bursts into flame. Includes handy ash shovel.

Singalong with the Mandrakes

Their cry may be instantly fatal, but boy can those Mandrakes nail a tune! Your whole family will be dying to listen to this double CD of karaoke classics, from 'Killing Me Softly' to 'I Won't Survive'.

SINGALONGA MANDRAKE!

My Little Hippogriff

Make believe with this truly magical creature – every girl's dream toy. Feed her, groom her, exercise her. But don't neglect or insult her, or she'll savage you. Unsuitable for children under eighteen years, due to razor-sharp parts.

Portaloo™ – the unique toilet-seat portkey

Travel to your workplace or school in comfort, and in an instant, with this fur-lined enchanted toilet seat. Works immediately on contact with bare buttock flesh.

The Death Eater's Cookbook

A medley of menacing menus from celebrity wizard chef Jamie Ollivander. From Voldemort Vol-au-vents to Crucio Cookies, these recipes are sure to hit the Dark Mark with your Death-Eating dinner guests.

Parselmouth Pun Page

Try these on your serpent friends –
they'll shed their skins laughing!
With thanks to S. Slytherin for the
translations.

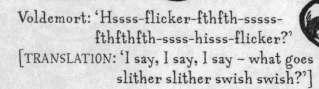

Voldemort: 'Hssss-flicker-fthfth-sssss-
          fthfthfth-ssss-hisss-flicker?'
[TRANSLATION: 'I say, I say, I say – what goes
          slither slither swish swish?']

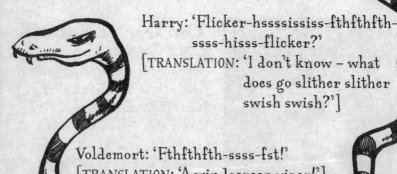

Harry: 'Flicker-hssssississ-fthfthfth-
        ssss-hisss-flicker?'
[TRANSLATION: 'I don't know – what
        does go slither slither
        swish swish?']

Voldemort: 'Fthfthfth-ssss-fst!'
[TRANSLATION: 'A windscreen viper!']

Nagini: 'Fss-flicker-sssss-fthfthfth-
flicker-ssss-hisss-fth.'
[TRANSLATION: 'My best snake friend is
frightfully good at sums.']

Basil the Basilisk: 'Fthss-sssshiss? Ssss-
fthfth-flickerflicker?'
[TRANSLATION: 'Oh, really? Why is that?']

Nagini: 'Ssss-fst-fthfthssss!'
[TRANSLATION: 'She's an adder!']

Voldemort: 'Hssss-flicker-fthfth-sssss-
flickerfthfth-ssss-hisss-fth?'
[TRANSLATION: 'I say, I say, I say – what
sports day event do snakes
always win?']

Harry: 'Flicker-hssssississ-flicker-
fthfthfth-ssss-hisss?'
[TRANSLATION: 'I don't know – what sports day
event do snakes always win?']

Voldemort: 'Fstsss-flickerssss-hisss!'
[TRANSLATION: 'The No-legged Race!']

For more forked-tongue fun, why not
join the Parselmouth Chatroom at
www.sssssssssssssssssssssssssss.com

77

What do American films and Harry's wand have in common?

They're both made in holly wood.

What amphibian haunts the girls' toilets at Hogwarts?

Moaning Turtle.

Why does Neville's toad, Trevor, keep disappearing?

He's got an Invisibility Croak.

Where would you find Dumbledore's Army?

Up his sleevey.

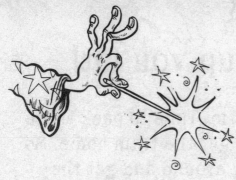

What do Hogwarts teachers use to correct pupils' homework?

Magic markers.

What are large and smelly, and come from another country?

Madame Maxime's trainers.

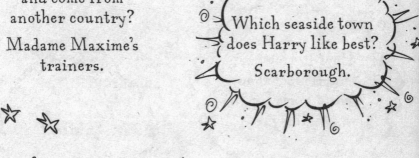

Which seaside town does Harry like best?

Scarborough.

Which side of Fluffy, the three-headed dog, is it best to stay on?

The outside.

Harry up you lot!

It's the end of term. Time to pack those wands away and get the train home. So stop pottering around and get the Hogwarts out of here!

How do Hogwarts pupils feel about going home for the holidays?

Chuffed!